NOTABLE JUDICIAL STANCES OVER INDIAN SOCIO-LEGAL ISSUES

TEJAS SATEESHA HINDER AND
VAISHNAVI SALIMATH

–VI of the IPC. The main accused was Barindra Kumar Ghose, who was a journalist and he started 'Jugantar', a Bengali weekly which soon resulted in a revolutionary organization. Barindra was alleged to have master minded the rebellion against the British Government in Bengal for independence. The rebellion involved preparation for armed militancy activities. The Court heard cases of all accused on merits and confirmed the conviction of the main accused and 11 other accused. Because the main accused was the leader of the society, he and 3 others who had manufactured bombs for the purpose were punished with transportation for life, whereas the others were given transportation for 10 years , 7 years etc. The charges of S-121 and S-122 were set aside in appeal but S-121A was upheld because there were evidences that Barindra and the others were collecting weapons for a far-off revolution and they 'wished' to be ready for it.

It was stated that 'Section 121 must be construed in its ordinary sense, and that its ambit is not necessarily restricted to overt acts including the collection of men, arms and ammunition.'

Thus, this case is an example of the situation in India when people were convicted for attacking or planning to attack the governmental institutions.

In ***Re: Cholancheri Ayammad and Ors. v. Unknown***(Moplah Rebellion case), there were 9 accused who were responsible for forming a mob of around 3000 people for a march. A small police force tried to stop them but around 100 of armed men including the 9 appellants murdered 2 constables and made the remaining policemen to retreat. Firstly, the trial court convicted the accused under S-121 of IPC and made it clear that "the actions of the insurgents need not, as a matter of evidence, be singled out individually in the crime committed - each of the accused who participated in the rebellion may be held guilty of waging war against the Government." So, the accused were convicted under S-121 read with S-34 of the IPC. In appeal made to Madras High Court, a preliminary objection was raised that requirements of S-196[4] of Cr.P.C. were not fulfilled which was rejected by the High Court. The main objection raised from the appellant's side was that the evidences against the accused were invalid. The arguments from the appellant's side was that the witnesses statements ought to have been rejected by the Court as they were being maliciously alleged to have committed the offence. The High Court concluded that though some of the evidences may be left out of consideration, but the main prosecution witnesses' statements which were of the policemen present at the scene cannot be considered to have been made out of enmity between them and the appellants. Thus, evidences were accepted and conviction was upheld.

Another major issue in the pre-independent scenario was whether under S-121, a war could be waged through speech and expression. In ***Emperor v. Hasrat Mohani,*** the accused was a Muslim and made a speech and through his speech tried to encourage members of his community to make and run similar institutions as that of the British Government. The question before the Bombay High Court was whether such speech would amount to the offence under S-121. The High Court held that for the offence of S-121 to be attracted, it must be clearly proved by the prosecution that such action is principally aimed at by the accused and not merely incidental. The High Court relied on the decision in ***Emperor v. Ganesh Damodar Savarkar*** in which the learned judge opined that "so long as a man (iii)The true criterion is the quo animo with which the gathering assembled;

(iv)The object of the gathering must be to attain by force and violence, an object of a general public nature, thereby striking directly against the King's authority;

(v) There is no distinction between principal and accessory and all who take part in the unlawful act incur the same guilt."[10]

In this case, the Nagpur High Court acquitted an appellant 'Mallu' who had been forced to join the attack on the police outposts and station-houses, and held that forced participation in an offence of such kind cannot make the person guilty of that offence.

The Court's interpretation makes the attack on a public property an essential ingredient in commission of an offence under S-121, but what about the situations where terrorists attack private institutions has not been answered.

In ***State vs Mohd. Afzal And Ors.***[11], there were four accused charged with various offences under the IPC, POTA[12] and the Explosive Substances Act, for attacking the Parliament in 2001 while it was in session. Accused no. 1 to 3 were charged with S-121 and S-120B for a conspiracy with 5 Pakistani terrorists with an intent to take hostage or kill the Prime Minister, Vice President and Members of Parliament. Mr. Ram Jethmalani was the counsel for the accused. Defending the accused from the charge of S-121, Mr. Jethmalani contended that 'war' cannot be defined with logical precision. According to him, the following attributes are pre-requisites for war :

"(i) An objective to over throw the government by conquest of territory or by compelling some form of conduct or establishing an ideology or form of government.

(ii) Means employed must be arms and ammunition and killing or overpowering of combatants, as distinct from killing civilians though they may be incidentally killed.

(iii) Number of participants, scale of violence and nature of operation should be on a sufficiently large scale.

(iv) A declaration by the competent executive authority of the State declaring a state of war."

As the act committed by the accused did not have the said attributes, it could be at best called a terrorist act. The counsel also stated that war is fought according to the rules of 'Hague Convention' and other covenants.

The Delhi High Court, however did not agree and stated that though these attributes make up for the definition of war in the real sense, this is not the only concept of war.. The High Court said : "190. Insurgency is treated to be an act of waging, war against the Government of India. We have dealt with what the Parliament of India means in the jural concept. It is the seat of the sovereignty of India. It symbolises the being of the Nation i.e. "India that is Bharat". A full blooded attack on the parliament when it is in Session would indeed be an act of war against the Government of India. The number of the combatants are only indicative of, certainly not determinative of, whether the attack would be an act of war. The five power available, to our mind, would be more decisive. To illustrate, a single person may have infiltrated into India with a nuclear bomb, a missile and a navigation system to guide a missile. He uses it to bomb the parliament when it is in Session and particularly when the President of India is to address it. The entire executive and the legislature is present. The President is there, the Vice-President is there, the Prime Minister, his entire cabinet is there. All members of Parliament are there. He intends by his attack to wipe out the entire legislative and executive body. This solitary act by one man would be more devastating then a 1000 armed men attacking the Parliament. Indeed, it would be an act of war.

191. Five or six heavily armed combatants who storm a public building, kill or take hostage civilians or for that matter highly respected citizens intend to only force the Government of India to concede to their demands. The act may not amount to waging war against the Government of India. But where the seat of the government of India itself is attacked, position would be entirely different. The two are uncomparable situations."

As for the charge of conspiracy, it was alleged by the accused that the charge was vague as there were no exact dates to be mentioned to point out conspiracy. The Court explained the meaning of conspiracy by stating that it is a feature of conspiracy that it is secret and thus not mentioning the exact dates is no vagueness at all.

The Court also explained S-120A and said that the mere agreement between two or more persons is the 'actus reus' and the intention to do the unlawful act is the 'mens rea'. A grey area regarding deciding on what did the co-conspirators contribute in furtherance of the common intention was decided by the Hon'ble Apex Court in ***State of Maharashtra and Ors. v. Som Nath Thapa and Ors.***It was observed by the Court "that for a person to conspire with another, he must have knowledge of what the co-conspirators were wanting to achieve and thereafter having the intent to further the illegal act takes recourse to a course of conduct to achieve the illegal end or facilitate its accomplishment. Except for extreme cases, intent could be inferred from knowledge for example whether a person was found in possession of an offending article, no legitimate use of which could be done by the offender. To illustrate, a person is found in possession of 100 Kg. of RDX, is proved to be visiting or visited by "A" against whom there is a charge of conspiring to blow up a public place. Here, the recovery of the offending article would be enough to infer a charge of conspiracy."

Finally, it was decided by the Delhi Court that with the fire power available with the accused, they could have wiped out the Indian Parliament, and accused no. 1 and 2 were active participants. Thus, the charge against the two under S-121 was upheld. As a result, they were also convicted under S-121A and also under S-122, S-302 read with S-120B and S-307 read with S-120B. As for the accused no. 3 i.e. S.A.R. Gilani, the only evidence presented by the prosecution was the list of telephone calls made by the accused no.1 and 2 to his phone and on the basis of such evidence, his guilt could not have been proved. The Court laid emphasis on the fact that for making a person liable for conspiracy, some participation has to be shown not necessarily some overt act but at least some circumstantial evidence. Thus, the charge was unsustainable according to the Court.

For accused no. 4 i.e. Afsan Guru (Navjot Sandhu), no evidence brought in by the prosecution could establish the involvement of her in the conspiracy. Thus, the Delhi High Court acquitted both accused no. 3 and 4 of all the charges.

In this case, it was made clear by the Court that attacking a public institution and killing innocents does not ipso facto amount to the offence of waging war under S-121.

The most important case regarding the subject is ***State (NCT of Delhi) v. Navjot Sandhu,***in which the Supreme Court went in detail to explain the scope of S-121. It was said that 'war' in S-121 is "not to be understood in international law sense of inter-country war involving military operations by and between two or more hostile countries. Apart from the legislative history of the provision and the understanding of the expression by various High Courts during the pre-independence days, the Illustration to Section 121 itself makes it clear that 'war' contemplated by Section 121 is not conventional warfare between two nations. Organizing or joining an insurrection against the Government of India is also a form of war. 'Insurrection' as defined in dictionaries and as commonly understood connotes a violent uprising by a group directed against the Government in power or the civil authorities."

The Supreme Court also put questions on the principles laid down in the ***Maganlal*** case. The first four principles were criticized by the Court that in today's context, such factors are of little or no value. It was also said that 'all objects of a general public nature' may not always amount to waging war under S-121. Thus, the scope of the provision was extended by the Apex Court. Afzal Guru's appeal was dismissed. Shaukat Hussain's appeal was partly allowed but he was still sentenced to life imprisonment under S-123 whereas the State's appeals against the acquittal of Gilani and Afsan Guru (Navjot Sandhu) were dismissed.

In***Md.Ajmal Md.Amir Kasab v. State Of Maharashtra***, the accused was one of the 10 terrorists who had attacked the Taj Hotel in Mumbai. Only the accused survived and the other 9 were killed by the Indian Security Forces. The analysis of this case is restricted to the question of the charge of S-121 although he was charged under various other sections of IPC and special laws. It was argued by the defense that the act committed by the accused could not be read as 'waging war against the Government of India' and the case is incomparable with that of State vs. Navjot Sandhu as in that case, the attack was on the Parliament building and in the present case, the attack was on CST Station which according to the defense was no more than a public building. The Supreme Court again laid emphasis on the fact that a terrorist act and an act of waging war may overlap each other. The Court further stated that: "What matters is that the attack was aimed at India and Indians. It was by foreign nationals. People were killed for no other reason than they were Indians; in case of foreigners, they were killed because their killing on Indian soil would embarrass India. The conspiracy, in furtherance of which the attack was made, was, inter alia, to hit at India; to hit at its financial centre; to try to give rise to communal tensions and create internal strife and insurgency; to demand that India should withdraw from Kashmir; and to dictate its relations with other countries. It was in furtherance of those objectives that the attack was made, causing the loss of a large number of people and injury to an even greater number of people. Nothing could have been more "in like manner and by like means as a foreign enemy would do". The court also rejected the arguments that death penalty be commuted as there was no fair trial and 'due process' was not followed. Also, the defense claimed that the High Court committed an error in balancing the aggravating and mitigating circumstances for awarding death sentence which were established in Machhi Singh v. State of Punjab which was rejected by the Court as it felt that the act had 'shook the collective conscience of the country'.

CHAPTER TWO

Speedy Trial

In a criminal trial, the judge , the litigants as well as the lawyers play integral roles when it comes to speedy disposal of cases. The arrears in the Indian Justice System have been ever increasing and expanding and have reached an alarming rate. Actions at various levels and effective measures must be taken so as to ensure disposal of cases in reasonable time while not affecting the quality of justice delivered.

Various committees have given recommendations from time to time to reduce inordinate delay in criminal proceedings. As already mentioned above, Cr.P.C has also been amended with a view to make the proceedings less time consuming. Alternative tribunals, special courts have also been established so as to reduce congestion in courts.

The Supreme Court at various instances has issued directions to the Center as well as the States to provide infrastructure to the Courts. The use of technology and modern tools has been realized by the Apex Court so as to make the system better. Attempts through judicial training have also been made so as to ensure judicial reforms, but it is disheartening to conclude that there still exists a mountain of arrears in the Courts today which has and is resulting in the denial of justice.

There are two sides to this. On one side, there are a large number of accused people who are detained and kept in prisons while awaiting the decisions of their respective trials and on the other hand, there are complaints of less number of convictions. The lawyers and the judges are the best to respond to such concerns.

The delay in such cases is an important concern as can be seen in various cases which have been decided or still in the process of trial for a period of more than 20, 30 and 40 years. The Supreme Court has played a pro- active role in ensuring the right of accused as well as victim to speedy trial but the main concern is that the said right must be recognized at the grass root level i.e. the Trial Court.

In *State of West Bengal v. Anwar Ali Sarkar*[1], a Bench of seven judges of the Supreme Court held that "the necessity of a speedy trial is too vague and uncertain to form the basis of valid and reasonable classification .It is too indefinite as there can hardly be any definite objective test to determine it. It is no classification at all in the real sense of the term as it is not based on any characteristics which are peculiar to persons or to cases which are to be subjected to the special procedure prescribed by the Act."

In *Machander v. State of Hyderabad*[2], the Supreme Court refused to remand the case back to the trial court for fresh trial because of delay of five years between the commission of the offence and the final judgment of the Supreme Court. The Supreme Court has categorically observed: "We are not prepared to keep persons on trial for their live and under indefinite suspense because trial judges omit to do their duty .... We have to draw a nice balance between conflicting rights and duties .... While it is incumbent on us to see that the guilty do not escape, it is even more necessary to see that the person accused of crimes are not indefinitely harassed .... While every reasonable latitude must be given to those concerned 'with the detection of crime and entrusted with administration of justice, but limits must be placed on the lengths to which they may go."

The Supreme Court in *Maneka Gandhi v. Union of India* [3]has stated clearly held that Article 21 of the Constitution of India confers a fundamental right on every individual not to be deprived of his life or personal liberty except according to procedure established by law and such procedure as required under Article 21 has to be "fair, just and reasonable" and not "arbitrary, fanciful or oppressive". The court has further stated that "If a person is deprived of his Liberty under a procedure which is not 'reasonable', 'fair' or 'just', such deprivation would be violative of his fundamental right under Article 21 and he would be entitled to enforce such fundamental right and secure his release." The apex Court has observed that in the broad sweep and content of Article 21 right to speedy trial is implicit.

The apex Court's decision in *Hussainara Khatoon(iv) v. Home Secretary, State of Bihar*[4] is a land mark in the development of speedy trial jurisprudence. In the instant case, a writ of habeas corpus was filed on behalf of men and women languishing in jails in the State of Bihar awaiting trial. Some of them had been in jail for a period much beyond what they would have spent had maximum sentence been imposed on them for the offence of which they were accused. Alarmed by the shocking revelations made in the writ petition and concerned about the denial of the basic human rights to those "victims of callousness of the legal and judicial system", Supreme Court went on to give a new direction to the Constitutional jurisprudence.

In doing so, the Court heavily relied on its decision in an earlier case in which the Court gave a very progressive interpretation to Article 21 of the Constitution. Taking this interpretation to its logical end, P.N. Bhagwati J., in Hussainara Khatoon's case said: "...Procedure prescribed by law for depriving a person of his liberty cannot be reasonable, fair or just unless that procedure ensures a speedy trial for determination of the guilt of such person. No procedure which does not ensure a reasonably quick trial can be regarded as 'reasonable, fair or just' and it would fall foul of Article 21. There can, therefore, be no doubt that speedy trial, and by speedy trial we mean reasonably expeditious trial, is an integral and essential part of the fundamental right to life and liberty enshrined in Article 21."

In *State of Bihar v. Uma Shankar Ketriwal,*[5] the High Court quashed the proceedings on the ground that the prosecution which commenced 16 years ago and still in progress, is an abuse of the process of the Court and should not be allowed to go further. Refusing to interfere with the decision of the High Court in the appeal, the Supreme Court said with regard to the delay that such protraction itself means considerable harassment to the accused and that there has to be a limit to the period for which criminal litigation is allowed to go on at the trial stage. The Court further observed that "We cannot lose sight of the fact that the trial has not made much headway even though no less than 20 years have gone by, such protection itself means considerably harassment to the accused not only monetarily but also by way of constant attention to the case and repeated appearances in Court, apart from anxiety. It may be said that the respondents themselves were responsible in a large manner for the slow pace of the case in as much as quite a few orders made by the trial Magistrate were challenged in higher Courts, but then there has to be a limit to the period for which criminal litigation is allowed to go on at the trial stage."

In *Raghubir Singh v. State of Bihar*,[6] a Bench of two judges of the Supreme Court held that the right to speedy trial is one of the dimensions of the fundamental right to life and liberty guaranteed by Article 21. The question whether the right to speedy trial has been infringed depends upon various factors. A host of question may arise for consideration: Was there delay? Was the delay inevitable having regard to the nature of the case? Was the delay unreasonable? Was the delay caused by the tactics of the defence? There may be other questions as well. But ultimately the question of infringement of the right to speedy justice is one of fairness in the administration of criminal justice even as 'acting fairly' is the essence of the principle of natural justice and "a fair and reasonable procedure" is what is contemplated by the expression "procedure established by law" in Article 21.

The most important decision regarding the issue is *Abdul Rahman Antulay v. R.S. Nayak*[7]. The Supreme Court gave a landmark decision and finally adjudicated upon the questions left open in Hussainara Khatoon's case, like the scope of the right, the circumstances in which it could be invoked, its consequences and limits etc. The salient features of the decision are as follows:

(a) Right to speedy trial flowing from Article 21 encompasses all the stages namely, the stage of investigation, inquiry, trial, appeal, revision and retrial.

(b) In every case, where right to speedy trial is alleged to have been infringed, the first question to be put and answered is who is responsible for the delay? Proceedings taken by either party in good faith, to vindicate their rights and interests, as perceived by them, cannot be taken as delaying tactic nor can the time taken in pursuing such proceedings be counted towards delay.

(c) While determining whether undue delay has occurred one must have regard to all the circumstances, including nature of offence, number of accused and witnesses, the workload of the Court concerned, prevailing local conditions and so on.

(d) Each and every delay does not necessarily prejudice the accused. However, inordinately long delay may be taken as presumptive proof of prejudice. Prosecution should not be allowed to become a persecution. But when does the prosecution become persecution, depends upon the facts of a given case.

(e) Accused's plea of denial of speedy trial cannot be defeated by saying that the accused didn't demand a speedy trial.

(f) The Court has to balance and weigh the several relevant factors- 'balancing test' and 'balancing processes – and determine in each case whether the right to speedy trial has been denied in a given case.

(g) Charge or conviction is to be quashed if the Court comes to the conclusion that right to speedy trial of an accused has been infringed. But this is not the only course open; it is open to the Court to make such other appropriate order – including an order to conclude the trial within a fixed time where the trial is not concluded or the sentence where the trial has concluded, as may be deemed just and equitable in the circumstances of the case.

(h) It is neither advisable nor practicable to fix any time limit for trial of offences because time required to complete trial of a case depends on the nature of the case.

(i) An objection based on denial of right to speedy trial and for relief on that account should first be addressed to the High Court. Even if the High Court entertains such a plea, ordinarily it should not stay the proceedings, except in a case of grave and exceptional nature. Such proceedings in High Court must be disposed of on a priority basis.

The Antulay judgment was followed in many following cases. But the Court realized in *"Common Cause" a Registered Society through its Director v. Union of India*[8]that many accused who are on trial for committing minor offences and do not have enough resources to furnish security or bond to secure bail languish in jails for a long period of time. Thus in this case, the Apex Court gave several guidelines as to when the accused may be released even on not furnishing bail bond if he has been in jail for a specific period while the trial is going on.

In *All India Judges' Association v. Union of India*[9], the apex Court held that it is a constitutional obligation of this Court to ensure that the backlog of cases is decreased and efforts are made to increase the disposal of cases. Apart from the steps which may be necessary for increasing the efficiency of the judicial officers, it appears that the time has come for protecting one of the pillars of the Constitution, namely, the judicial system, by directing increase in the judges strength from the existing ratio of judge-population ratio.

All these cases show that even after recognizing the right to speedy trial, there is not much improvement in reality. Justice is served but after a long period of time which may be as long as 40-50 years. Thus, all those who participate in a trial are responsible.

In all the above mentioned cases, the sorry conditions existed because in some cases, either there is vacancy of judges, the police does not complete the investigation in time, the lawyers ask for dates for petty reasons, the accused himself causes delay.

[1] AIR 1952 SC 75

[2] AIR 1955 SC 792.

[3] (1978) 1 SCC 248.

[4] (1980) 1 SCC 81.

[5] (1981) 3 SCC 610

[6] AIR 1987 SC 149

[7] (1992) 1 SCC 225

[8] (1996) 4 SCC 33.

[9] (2002) 4 SCC 247.

CHAPTER THREE

Film-makers and Censorship

The High Courts and the Apex Court of India by way of many judgments over the time have safeguarded the rights of the country's people. The right to freedom of speech and expressions is also included in the list of several rights guaranteed by the Constitution of India.

The Supreme Court dealt with the issue of constitutionality of censorship of the Cinematograph Act, 1952 for the first time in ***K.A. Abbas v. Union of India*[1]** in which the Apex Court decided in favour of the 1952 Act and upheld its constitutionality giving reasons that it falls under the ambit of 'reasonable restrictions' under Article-19(2). The reasoning given by the Court was that films are a different class of art or expression because it can affect emotions of people deeper than any other form. At the same time the Court cautioned that "If the regulations venture into something which goes beyond this legitimate opening to restrictions, they can be questioned on the ground that a legitimate power is being abused."[2]

Another landmark case in this regard is of ***S.Rangarajan v. P.Jagjivan Ram*[3]** In this case, an appeal was filed by the makers of the National Award winning film 'Ore Oru

Gramathile' in the Apex Court against the decision of the High Court of Madras of revoking the 'U-Certificate'. The film talked about the sufferings of Brahmins in Tamil Nadu due to reservations in jobs, while also using some words against Dr. Ambedkar. The decision of the High Court was overruled by the Supreme Court thus upholding the right to freedom of speech and expression, saying that a film is the best and most important source of discussing issues related to society and public in general. Thus, the maker has the right to express his/her views on a particular subject even if others or State don't approve of it. To put it in simple words, open discussion is an integral part of the democratic structure and it cannot be taken away by anyone arbitrarily.

Court also held in the same case that the grounds mentioned under A-19 (2) must have direct nexus with the expression. It cannot be out of the ordinary and it is the State's duty to make sure that the freedom of speech and expression is protected and it must be able to handle a hostile situation.

In ***Life Insurance Corporation of India v. Prof. Manubhai D. Shah[4]***, the Supreme Court held that criticizing the State Government cannot be a reason to not allow to make public exhibition of the film. (a non-feature film on Bhopal Gas Disaster).

In the case of the controversial movie 'The Da Vinci Code', a writ petition filed by the AICWA (All India Christians Welfare Association) was rejected by the Apex Court saying that the movie had been running in various Christian countries and there was no point of any objection. Some states that had banned the movie were found to be irrational and the High Courts in those respective states imposed costs on those Governments and quashed the bans, upholding the right of speech and expression.

In ***Sree Raghavendra Films v. Government of Andhra Pradesh[5]***, the screening of film 'Bombay' was suspended (even after given the go-ahead by the Censor Board) under S-8(1) of the A.P. Cinemas Regulation Act of 1955. The reasons given were that it could hurt the sentiments of some particular groups. It was found by the Court the order passed by the authorities was irrational and arbitrary because the movie was not watched by the ones who passed an order against its exhibition. Thereby, the Court quashed the order.

[1] AIR 1971 SC 481

[2] AIR 1971 SC 481

[3] (1989) 2 SCC 574

[4] AIR 1993 SC 171

[5] 1995 (2) ALD 81

CHAPTER FOUR

Custodial Jurisprudence

Joginder Kumar v. State of U.P.

Citation: 1994 AIR 1349, 1994 SCC (4) 260

Court: Supreme Court of India

Facts

This was a petition under Article 32 of the Constitution of India. The petitioner was a young man of 28 years of age who had completed his LL.B. and had enrolled himself as an advocate. The Senior Superintendent of Police, Ghaziabad, Respondent 4 called the petitioner in his office for making enquiries in some case. The petitioner on 7-1-1994 at about 10 o'clock appeared personally along with his brothers Shri Mangeram Choudhary, Nahar Singh Yadav, Harinder Singh Tewatia, Amar Singh and others before Respondent 4. Respondent 4 kept the petitioner in his custody. When the brother of the petitioner made enquiries about the petitioner, lie was told that the petitioner will be set free in the evening after making some enquiries in connection with a case. On 7-1-1994 at about 12.55 p.m., the brother of the petitioner being apprehensive of the intentions of Respondent 4, sent a telegram to the Chief Minister of U.P. apprehending his brother's implication in some criminal case and also further apprehending the petitioner being shot dead in fake encounter. In spite of the frequent enquiries, the whereabouts of the petitioner could not be located. On the evening of 7-1- 1994, it came to be known that petitioner is detained in illegal custody of 5th respondent, SHO, P.S. Mussoorie.

Question arose

- Whether the private rights of an individual superseded the protection of society.

Considering the increase in crime and human rights violations by way of indiscriminate arrests, the Hon'ble Court sought a way to strike a balance between the two.

Judgment

It was held by a three-judge bench of Supreme Court that an arrest cannot simply be made because a police officer has been conferred with this particular power. There remained a difference between the power to arrest and justification for the exercise of this power.

Mere allegation of an offence is not a reason good enough to make an arrest of the person. Similarly, a reasonable belief is not enough for a person to be arrested by a police officer, keeping in mind the constitutional rights granted to the person. It was also held that Articles 21 and 22(1) of the Constitution should be protected and recognized.

For the effective enforcement of these fundamental rights, an arrested person being held in custody is entitled, if he so requests, to have one friend relative or other person, who is known to him or likely to take an interest in his welfare, be told, as far as is practicable, that he has been arrested and where is he being detained. An entry shall be required to be made in the Diary as to who was informed of the arrest. These protections from power must be held to flow from Articles 21 and 22(1) and enforced strictly.

Further in this case, the Third Report of National Police Commission was cited, which mentioned power of arrest as one of the chief sources of corruption in the police and suggested that a staggering number of arrests (nearly 60%) were either unnecessary or unjustified and that such unjustified police action accounted for 43.2% of the expenditure of the jails.

The **3rd Report of the National Police Commission** observed:

"An arrest during the investigation of a cognizable case may be considered justified in one or other of the following circumstances:

(i) The case involves a grave offence like murder, dacoity, robbery, rape etc., and it is necessary to arrest the accused and bring his movements under restraint to infuse confidence among the terror stricken victims.

(ii) The accused is likely to abscond and evade the processes of law.

(iii) The accused is given to violent behavior and is likely to commit further offences unless his movements are brought under restraint.

(iv) The accused is a habitual offender and unless kept in custody he is likely to commit similar offences again."

The Supreme Court held that right of an arrested person upon request, to have someone informed about his arrest and right to consult privately with lawyers are inherent in Articles 21 and 22 of the Constitution. The Supreme Court observed that no arrest can be made because it is lawful for the Police officer to do so. The existence of the power to arrest is one thing. The justification for the exercise of it is quite another. The Police Officer must be able to justify the arrest apart from his power to do so. Arrest and detention in police lock-up of a person can cause incalculable harm to the reputation and self-esteem of a person. No arrest should be made by Police Officer without a reasonable satisfaction reached after some investigation as to the genuineness and bona fides of a complaint and a reasonable belief both as to the person's complicity and even so as to the need to effect arrest.

The Supreme Court issued the following requirements:

1. An arrested person being held in custody is entitled, if he so requests, to have one friend, relative or other person who is known to him or likely to take an interest in his welfare told as far as practicable that he has been arrested and where is being detained.
2. The Police Officer shall inform the arrested person when he is brought to the police station of this right.
3. An entry shall be required to be made in the Diary as to who was informed of the arrest.

These protections from power must be held to flow from Articles 21 and 22 (1) and enforced strictly.

Smt Nilabati Behera alias Lalita Behera v. State Of Orissa And Others

Citation: AIR 1993 SC 1960

Court: Supreme Court of India

Brief Facts

Smt. Nilabati Behera alias Lalita Behera addressed a letter to the Supreme Court of the country which was treated as a petition under Article 32 of the Indian Constitution for determining the claim of compensation made therein consequent upon, the death of petitioner's son, Suman Behera, in police custody. Suman Behera was taken to the police custody in connection with an investigation of an offence of theft and detained at the police outpost. On the next day, the petitioner came to know that the dead body of his son was found at the railway station. There were multiple injuries on the body of Suman Behera and it was obvious that this death has been caused because of such injuries and it was an unnatural death.

Issue

The allegation made is that it is a case of custodial death since Suman Behera died as a result of the multiple injuries inflicted to him while he was in police custody, and thereafter his dead body was thrown on the railway track. The prayer made in the petition is for the award of compensation to the petitioner, the mother of Suman Behera, for contravention of the fundamental right to life guaranteed under Article 21 of the Constitution.

Arguments of Additional Solicitor General on behalf of state

Additional Solicitor General made an argument that the factual foundation for a liability of the State is absent in the present case. The defence of the respondents is that Suman Behera managed to escape from police custody at about 3 a.m. on the night between the 1st and 2nd December 1987 from the Police Outpost Jeraikela, where he was detained and guarded by Police Constable; he could not be apprehended thereafter in spite of a search; and the dead body of Suman Behera was found on the railway track the next day with multiple injuries which indicated that he was run over by a passing train after he had escaped from police custody. In short, on this basis, the allegation of custodial death was denied and consequently the respondents' responsibility for the unnatural death of Suman Behera.

Arguments of amicus curiae for the petitioner

It was contended that the evidence adduced during the inquiry does not support the defence of respondents and there is no reason to reject the finding of the learned District Judge that Suman Behera died in police custody as a result of injuries inflicted upon him

Ratio

(Authored by J S Verma)

It is significant that there is no cogent independent evidence of any search made by the police to apprehend Suman Behera if the defence of his escape from police custody is true. On the contrary, after the discovery of the dead body on the railway track in the morning by some railway men, it was much later in the day that the police reached the spot to take charge of the dead body. This conduct of the concerned police officers is also a significant circumstance to assess the credibility of the defence version. It was stated by the doctor that while all the injuries could not be caused in a train accident, it was possible to cause all the injuries by lathi blows.

There is a difference between the liability of the state in public law and the liability of the state in private law for payment of compensation in action on tort. It may be mentioned straightaway that award of compensation in a proceeding under Article 32 by this court or by the High Court under Article 226 of the Constitution is a remedy available in public law, based on strict liability for contravention of fundamental rights to which the principle of sovereign immunity does not apply, even though it may be available as a defence in private law in an action based on tort.

The Court is not helpless and the wide powers given to this Court by Article 32, which itself is a fundamental right, imposes a constitutional obligation on this Court to forge such new tools, which may be necessary for doing complete justice and enforcing the fundamental rights guaranteed in the Constitution, which enable the award of monetary compensation in appropriate cases, where that is the only mode of redress available. The power available to this Court under Article 142 is also an enabling provision in this behalf.

Concurring opinion of Justice Dr Anand

It is an obligation of the State, to ensure that there is no infringement of the indefeasible rights of a citizen to life, except in accordance with law while the citizen is in its custody. The precious right guaranteed by Article 21 of the Constitution of India cannot be denied to convicts, under trials or other prisoners in custody, except according to procedure established by law. There is a great responsibility on the police or prison authorities to ensure that the citizen in its custody is not deprived of his right to life. His liberty is in the very nature of things circumscribed by the very fact of his confinement and therefore his interest in the limited liberty left to him is rather precious. The duty of care on the part of the State is strict and admits of no exceptions. The wrongdoer is accountable and the State is responsible if the person in custody of the police is deprived of his life except according to the procedure established by law.

Held

The Supreme Court directed the respondent-State of Orissa to pay the sum of Rs.1,50,000 to the petitioner and a further sum of Rs.10,000 as to be paid to the Supreme Court Legal Aid Committee.

D.K. Basu v. State of West Bengal

Citation: (1997) 1 SCC 416

Court: The Supreme Court of India

The Hon'ble Supreme Court laid down specific guidelines that are required to be followed while making arrests, the same have been listed below:

I. The police personnel carrying out the arrest and handling the interrogation of the arrestee should bear accurate, visible and clear identification and name tags with their designations. The particular of all such personnel who handle interrogation of the arrestee must be recorded in a register.

II. That the police officer carrying out the arrest shall prepare a memo of arrest *(sample provided later)* at the time of arrest and such memo shall be attested by at least one witness, who may be either a member of the family of the arrestee or a respectable person of the locality from where the arrest is made. It shall also be counter signed by the arrestee and shall contain the time and date of arrest.

III. A person who has been arrested or detained and is being held in custody in a police station or interrogation centre or other lock up, shall be entitled to have one friend or relative or other person known to him or having interest in his welfare being informed, as soon as practicable, that he has been arrested and is being detained at the particular place, unless the attesting witness of the memo of arrest is himself such a friend or a relative of the arrestee.

IV. The time, place of arrest and venue of custody of an arrestee must be notified by the police where the next friend or relative of the arrestee lives outside the district or town through the Legal Aid Organization in the District and the police station of the area concerned telegraphically within a period of 8 to 12 hours after the arrest.

V. The person arrested must be made aware of his right to have someone informed of his arrest or detention as soon as he is put under arrest or is detained.

VI. An entry must be made in the diary at the place of detention regarding the arrest of the person which shall also disclosed the name of the next friend of the person who has been informed of the arrest and the names and particulars of the police officials in whose custody the arrestee is.

VII. The arrestee should, where he so request, be also examined at the time of his arrest and major and minor injuries, if any present on his /her body, must be recorded at that time. The Inspector's Memo must be signed both by the arrestee and the police officer effecting the arrest and its copy provided to the arrestee.

VIII. The arrestee should be subjected to medical examination by a trained doctor every 48 hours during his detention in custody by a doctor on the panel of approved doctor appointed by Director, Health Services of the concerned State or Union Territory, Director, Health Services should prepare such a panel for all Tehsils and Districts as well.

IX. Copies of all the documents including the memo of arrest, referred to above, should be sent to the Magistrate for his record.

X. The arrestee may be permitted to meet his lawyer during interrogation, though not throughout the interrogation.

XI. A police control room should be provided at all district and State headquarters where information regarding the arrest and the place of custody of the arrestee shall be communicated by the officer causing the arrest, within 12 hours of effecting the arrest and at the police control room it should be displayed on a conspicuous notice board.

Muhabath Beevi v. Mrs.Vasantha

Citation: Cont.Petn.No.16 of 2008 in Crime No.11 of 2007

Court: Madurai Bench of Madras High Court

Bench: K Chandru J.

Case Overview

This Contempt Petition filed under Section 11 of Contempt of Courts Act, 1971 for the alleged willful disobedience of the guidelines issued by the Hon'ble Supreme Court of India in D.K. Basu v. State of West Bengal.

Facts

The case of the petitioner was that on 23.09.2007, around 4.30 a.m. the respondent came with a posse of 12 policemen and arrested her, that too when she was offering her prayer being the month of Ramalass. She was not allowed to wear her saree and dragged to the police station with her lungi. No arrest memo was given to her near relatives. She was also not given the grounds of arrest and was not allowed to meet her relatives, friend or an Advocate. No diary entry was made about her arrest immediately. She was produced before the Judicial Magistrate No.1, Ramanathapuram, around 6.30 p.m. On her complaint regarding her health condition she was sent for medical treatment at the Government Hospital around 7.00 p.m. The arrest memo was given to her brother Likat Ali Khan, at 2.00 p.m showing as if she was arrested at 11.30 a.m. near the Bus Stand.

Aggrieved by this conduct and blatant violation of guidelines given in the D.K.Basu's case, she has filed the present contempt petition. Statutory notice was ordered on 11.01.2008. Pursuant to which the respondent appeared before this court 11.02.2008. The respondent has filed three counter affidavits dated 01.02.2008, 04.02.2008 and 19.08.2008. She had also produced certain documents in support of her case.

On the side of the petitioner, a supporting affidavit from Likat Ali Khan, the brother of the petitioner, has been filed.

He was the person to whom the arrest memo was given by the respondent. This Court ordered to produce the records from the Judicial Magistrate.1, Ramanathapuram, in Crime No.11 of 2007, which was accordingly received by the Registry and circulated to this Court. This Court also directed the respondent to produce the case diary before this Court, by an order dated 12.08.2008. The respondent was also directed to be present before this Court on 28.08.2008 onwards and the respondent was also present.

From a perusal of all the records, including the case diary and the Court file, it clearly shows that the respondent has violated the guidelines, more particularly, the guidelines No.2 & 7, while arresting the petitioner.

The counter affidavit filed by the respondent is only an attempt to cover up the violations of D.K. Basu guidelines. Though the respondent claims that the petitioner was arrested at 11.30 p.m. near the bus stand, it is only a fabrication of the records. As seen from the supporting affidavit, the arrest was made around 4.30 a.m. in the house of the petitioner. There is no reason as to why the petitioner should be found loitering near the bus stand around 11.30 a.m. at the time of her arrest as suggested by the respondent.

The other allegation that she was dragged from her house and was not allowed to wear her saree is also proved, since there was no denial by the respondent regarding the attire worn by the petitioner during the arrest.

The respondent fairly admitted that the petitioner was sent for medical treatment only after the remand made by J.M.I and that too, around 7.00 p.m. She has no explanation as to how this answer could have been given in the arrest memo which according to her was handed over to the near relative i.e. Likat Ali Khan around 11.30 a.m. Obviously, it is a false statement made by the respondent and to cover up her disobedience of the D.K. Basu guidelines. This one ground of violation is sufficient to punish the respondent in this contempt petition. Apart from disobeying the Supreme Court's guidelines, she has also produced false documents before this Court, thereby, aggravating her culpability.

Order

The prayer in the Contempt Petition was to punish the respondent contemner for the deliberate and willful disobedience of the guidelines issued by the Supreme Court in D.K.Basu v. State of West Bengal.

In that case, the Supreme Court in Para 36 of its judgment gave 11 guidelines which are required to be followed, in case of arrest or detention. These 11 guidelines have now widely come to be known as the 11 Commandments to be implemented by a Station House Officer. The guidelines No.2 and 7 are usefully extracted for the case on hand:-

"2. That the police officer carrying out the arrest of the arrestee shall prepare a memo of arrest at the time of arrest and such memo shall be attested by at least one witness, who may be either member of the family of the arrestee or a respectable person of the locality from where the arrest is made. It shall also be countersigned by the arrestee and shall contain the time and date of arrest.

7. The arrestee should, where he so requests, be also examined at the time of his arrest and major and minor injuries, if any, present on his/her body, must be recorded at that time. The "Inspection Memo" must be signed both by the arrestee and the police officer effecting the arrest and its copy provided to the arrestee."

The Supreme Court also gave directions as to what should be done for the violation of these guidelines by any Officer of the Police and it is out in paragraph nos 37 and 38. The same is usefully extracted below:-

"37. Failure to comply with the requirements hereinabove mentioned shall apart from rendering the concerned official liable for departmental action, also render him liable to be punished for contempt of Court and the proceedings for contempt of Court may be instituted in any High Court of the country, having territorial jurisdiction over the matter.

38. The requirements, referred to above flow from Articles 21 and 22(1) of the Constitution and need to be strictly followed. These would apply with equal force to the other governmental agencies also to which a reference has been made earlier."

CHAPTER FIVE

Manual Scavenging

Judiciary on the other hand has always played an active role in strengthening the cause of socio-economic welfare by translating several directive principles into enforceable rights for the upliftment of poor and weaker section of the society.[1] A liberal interpretation of article 21 of the constitution has created numerous rights and has given a new direction to social welfare jurisprudence in India. With regard to judicial response towards the manual scavengers, recently courts have adopted a stern attitude towards the manual scavenging and pulled up the State authorities for failing to eliminate manual scavenging.

Safai Karamchari Andolan v. Union of India[2]

In the present case the Supreme Court acknowledged the menace of manual scavenging in India as an inhuman, degrading and undignified profession. The Supreme Court observed that PEMSR Act, 2013 and the EMSCDL Act, 1993 neither dilutes constitutional mandate of article 17 of the constitution nor does it condone inaction on part of union and state governments under EMSCDL Act, 1993. The Supreme Court held that the PEMSR Act, 2013 expressly acknowledges article 17 and 21 of the constitution as the rights of persons engaged in sewage cleaning and cleaning tanks as well persons cleaning human excretion on railway tracks.

Supreme Court laid down following propositions with regards to rehabilitation of manual scavengers:

i. If the practice of manual scavenging has to be brought to a close and also to prevent future generations from the inhuman practice of manual scavenging, rehabilitation of manual scavengers will need to include: (a) Sewer deaths – entering sewer lines without safety gears should be made a crime even in emergency situations. For each such death, compensation of Rs. 10 lakhs should be given to the family of the deceased. (b) Railways – should take time bound strategy to end manual scavenging on the tracks. (c) Persons released from manual scavenging should not have to cross hurdles to receive what is their legitimate due under the law. (d) Provide support for dignified livelihood to safai karamchari women in accordance with their choice of livelihood schemes.

v. Identify the families of all persons who have died in sewerage work (manholes, septic tanks) since 1993 and award compensation of Rs.10 lakhs for each such death to the family members depending on them. ii. Rehabilitation must be based on the principles of justice and transformation. Supreme Court stressed on the rehabilitation of manual scavengers in accordance with part IV of the PEMSR Act, 2013. The Supreme Court directed the state governments and union territories to fully implement various provisions of PEMSR Act, 2013 and take appropriate action for non-implementation as well as violation of provisions contained in PEMSR Act, 2013.

Delhi Jal Board v. National Campaign for Dignity & Rights of Sewerage & Allied Workers[3]

In the present case, the Supreme Court passed a landmark judgement identifying and highlighting the apathy and plight of the disadvantaged sections of the society, particularly the scavengers and sewage workers, who risk their lives by going down the drainage without any safety equipment and security and have been deprived of fundamental rights to equality, life and liberty for last more than six decades.

The Supreme Court also criticised the government and the state apparatus on being insensitive to the safety and wellbeing of those who are, on account of sheer poverty, compelled to work under most unfavourable conditions and regularly face the threat of being deprived of their life. Supreme Court also snubbed the elitist mindset of the wealthy class with regard to public interest litigation / Pro Bono litigation. The Supreme Court not only directed to pay higher compensation to the families of the deceased, but also directed the civic bodies to ensure immediate compliance of the directions and orders passed by the Delhi High Court for ensuring safety and security of the sewage workers.

[1] Samuel D. Permutt, The Manual Scavenging Problem: A Case for the Supreme Court of India, 20 Cardozo J. Int'l & Comp. L. 277 (2011-2012)

[2] 2014 (4) SCALE 165

[3] 2011 (8) SCC 568

CHAPTER SIX

Parliamentary Privileges

GK Reddy Case

One of the earliest instances when a conflict arose in India was in the case *Gunupati Keshavrom Reddi v Nafisul Hasan.*[1] There was confusion on the question of whether the fundamental rights control in any way the privileges which the House enjoys under Art 105(3).[2] A certain Homi Mistry was arrested at his Bombay residence under a warrant issued by the Speaker of the Uttar Pradesh Assembly for contempt of the House and was flown to Lucknow and kept in the Speaker's custody in a hotel. On his application for a writ of habeas corpus, the Supreme Court directed his release as he had not been produced before a magistrate within 24 hours of his arrest as provided in Art 22(2). This decision, therefore, indicated that Art I94 (or Art 105) was subject to the Articles of Part III of the Constitution.[3]

Searchlight Case

The next landmark case was *The Searchlight* case.[4] Pandit Sharma, the petitioner in the case, was editor of an English daily newspaper, *Searchlight,* in Patna. He invited the wrath of the Legislative Assembly of Bihar by publishing extracts from proceedings of the Legislative Assembly including extracts that the Speaker had been ordered to be expunged. The Speaker had referred the matter to the Privileges Committee of the Assembly, which in turn issued a show cause notice to the petitioner. Pandit Sharma approached the Supreme Court under Art 32 of the Constitution, and alleged that the proceedings initiated by the Assembly violated his fundamental right of speech and expression under Art 19(I)(a) of the Constitution. In support of his contention the petitioner relied on *Gunupati v Naffsul Hasan.[5]*It was held that the powers, privileges and immunities available in terms of Arts 105(3) and 194(3) stood in the same supreme position as the provisions of Part III of the Constitution (the fundamental rights chapter) and therefore the principle of harmonious construction had to be adopted.[6] The court concluded that the fundamental right of free speech and expression under Art 19(I)(a), as it is being general in nature, must yield to Art 194(1) and the latter part of Art 194(3) which are special provisions.

Keshav Singh's Case

The question whether courts can interfere with the power of a Legislature to commit for its contempt arose most dramatically in the *Keshav Singh's* case.[7] The case may be regarded as the high-water mark of legislative-judiciary conflict in a privilege matter in which the relationship between the two was brought to a very critical point; and the whole episode was reminiscent of the conflict between the House of Commons and the judiciary in England in the 17th century.[8]

The facts leading to the reference to the Supreme Court bythe President were as follows. Keshav Singh printed and published a pamphlet against a member of the Uttar Pradesh State Legislative Assembly. The House found him guilty of contempt and sentenced him to be reprimanded. When the Speaker administered a reprimand to him, he behaved in an objectionable manner. Accordingly, the House committed him to imprisonment for seven days for contempt. The warrant of committal did not contain the facts constituting the alleged contempt. Keshav Singh moved a petition, under Art 226 of the Constitution, through his advocate and challenged his committal as being a breach of his fundamental rights. Adivision bench of the High Court sitting at Lucknow gave notice to the government counsel and on the appointed day proceeded to hear the application for bail. The government counsel did not appear and the division bench heard the application and ordered the release of Keshav Singh on interim bail pending a decision on his writ petition. The Legislative Assembly found Keshav Singh and his advocate in moving the High Court, and the two judges of the High Court in entertaining the petition, guilty of contempt of the Legislative Assembly. The Assembly passed a resolution that all of them, including the two High Court judges, be produced before it in custody. The High Court judges and the advocate in question then filed writ petitions before the High Court at Allahabad. Afull bench of the High Court admitted the writ petitions and ordered a stay of execution of the Assembly's resolution. Subsequently, the Assembly passed a clarificatory resolution modifying its earlier stand

and asking the judges and the advocate to appear before the House and offer their explanations. Thus there emerged a complete legislative-judiciary deadlock.[9] At this stage, the President of India referred the matter to Supreme Court for its advisory opinion under Art 143(1). The advisory opinion given by a Constitution Bench comprising of seven judges of the Supreme Court is by far the most elaborate discourse on matters relating to powers, privileges and immunities of the legislatures under the Constitution of India.

By a majority of six to one, the Supreme Court held that the two judges had not committed contempt of the Legislature by issuing the bail order. The court held that the conduct of the judges could not be discussed in any House under Art 211 of the Constitution.[10] The court also held that the right of citizens to move the judicature and the right of advocates to assist that process must remain uncontrolled by Art 105(3). This is necessary to enforce of the fundamental rights and to sustaining the rule of law in this country.[11]

Raja Ram Pal Case

The present position in the law of parliamentary privileges has been laid down in the case of *Raja Ram Pal v The Honourable Speaker, Lok Sabha, &* Ors.[12] The Supreme Court has extensively dwelled on the matter and has delivered a judgment which is by far the most comprehensive decision in this field of law. After considering the various issues raised by the parties, Y. K. Sabarwal CJ, writing the majority judgment for himself and Balakrishnan and D. K. Jain JJ. formulated the following issues for determination:[13]

1. Does the court, within the constitutional scheme, have the jurisdiction to decide the content and scope of powers, privileges and immunities of the Legislatures and its members?
2. If the first question is answered in the affirmative, can it be found that the powers and privileges of the Legislatures in India, in particular with reference to Article 105, include the power of expulsion of their members?
3. In the event of such power of expulsion being found, does the court have the jurisdiction to interfere in the exercise of the said power or privilege conferred on the Parliament and its members or Committees and, if so, is this jurisdiction circumscribed by certain limits?

Regarding the first issue, although both the parties involved conceded the jurisdiction of the court to interpret Art 105, the court nevertheless decided to enter into a detailed discussion on the matter. Having established that the court has jurisdiction to examine the scope and nature of the powers, privileges and immunities enjoyed by the legislatures in India, the Court then addressed the second issue and examined whether such powers and privileges included the power of expulsion.

The court felt that the two organs, namely the legislature and the judiciary, must function, rationally, harmoniously and in a spirit of understanding within their respective spheres. Thus the court ventured to lay down certain parameters for the judicial review of actions by the legislatures in the exercise of the powers under Art 105 or Art 194. These principles, it is felt, will remove ambiguity regarding the jurisdiction of the courts in relation to parliamentary privileges.[14]

Contrast the willingness of the Supreme Court in *Raja Ram Pal* to bend over backwards with its approach in *PV. Narasimha Rao* less than a decade ago.[15] In 1993, a no-confidence motion against the then Prime Minister Narashima Rao threatened the existence of his government. With an intent to defeat the motion, Rao and his senior cabinet colleagues bribed 10 members of the Lower House to have them vote against the no-confidence motion. Nine members complied while one member, having accepted the bribe, abstained from voting. Charges were filed at the trial court against all bribe givers and takers under the *Prevention of Corruption Act, 1988 ('PCA')* read along with the provisions relating to criminal conspiracy under the *Indian Penal Code, 1872.* A petition to quash the charges framed by the trial court having been rejected by the High Court, the appellants approached the Supreme Court. Their actions, the appellants claimed, were privileged under Article 105(2): "No Member of Parliament shall be liable to any proceedings in any court in respect of anything said or any vote given by him in Parliament or any committee thereof, and no person shall be so liable in respect of the publication by or under the authority of either House of Parliament of any report, papers, votes or proceedings." By a majority of 3:2, the Supreme Court immunized bribe takers against prosecution for their alleged crimes.

In concluding that the bribe takers enjoyed immunity under Article 105(2), Bharucha J. emphasized the broad character of protection, being "in respect of" anything said or any vote given.[16] The broad protection, according to him, was "absolute and necessary," given the role Members of Parliament perform.[17]

[1] Gunupati Keshavrom Reddi v Nafisul Hasan AIR 1954 SC 636

[2] Or under Art 194 which is the corresponding Article relating to state legislatures.

[3] Shukla, V. N., Constitution of India, p. 391. (Eastern Book Company 10th Edn 2002)

[4] M. S. M. Sharma v Shri Krishan Sinha AIR 1959 SC 395

[5] Gunupati Keshavrom Reddi v Nafisul Hasan AIR 1954 SC 636

[6] M. S. M. Sharma v Shri Krishan Sinha AIR 1959 SC 395, p. 410

[7] Powers, Privileges and Immunities of State Legislatures, Re, AIR 1965 SC 745.

[8] Jain, M. P., Indian Constitutional Law, p. 68 (Wadhwa & Company, 4th edn 2002)

[9] Jain, M. P., Indian Constitutional Law, p. 69 (Wadhwa & Company, 4th edn 2002)

[10] Article 211 (and 121 in the case of the Parliament) mandates that no discussion shall take place in the legislature with respect to the conduct of any judge of the Supreme Court or of the High Court in the discharge of his duties.

[11] Jain, M. P., Indian Constitutional Law, p. 69 (Wadhwa & Company, 4th edn 2002)

[12] Raja Ram Pal v The Honourable Speaker, Lok Sabha, & Ors (2007) 3 SCC 184

[13] ibid, para 36.

[14] V. Shyam Kishore, Parliamentary Privileges and the Judiciary - A Search for the Common Ground, 33 Commw. L. Bull. 443 (2007)

[15] PV Narsimha Rao v State (1998) 4 SCC 626

[16] Ibid, para 109

[17] Shubhankar Dam, Parliamentary Privileges as Facade: Political Reforms and the Indian Supreme Court,

2007 Sing. J. Legal Stud. 162 (2007)

9 798890 023728

Printed by Libri Plureos GmbH in Hamburg,
Germany